Spirituali'

'Of Lions, Rats, Wi.

Anthony Buckley

Vicar of St John's, Folkstone

GROVE BOOKS LIMITED

RIDLEY HALL RD CAMBRIDGE CB3 9HU

Contents

The Cover Illustration is by Peter Ashton

First Impression May 2001
ISSN 0262-799X
ISBN 1 85174 465 7

1
Asking the Right Questions

Stories challenge us. They challenge us to take sides with the characters: Do I want this person to win or lose? Do I want the bad guys punished or forgiven? Do I want the good guys to be arrogant or magnanimous? They also challenge on a deeper level: What do these decisions say about me? The author may set out to portray one character as heroic, another as villainous. Do I share the author's moral framework and judgments? Do I agree with the underlying perceptions and standards that are expressed here?

These challenges are as present in Ladybird books or Agatha Christie as they are in *Pilgrim's Progress*. We never simply process the words of a book like some sort of computer scanner. We are involved, making continual conscious or sub-conscious choices about the characters, the author and ourselves.

These are important questions. The answers both reflect and shape our personality.

The Diocese of Canterbury Spirituality Group defines spirituality as 'Our whole life lived in relation to God.'[1] This broad definition reminds us that our leisure, including reading books and watching films, has something to do with our relationship with God. The questions mentioned above express an underlying spiritual question: Is there anything in this story that increases my understanding of faith, of God, or of human response to him?

This booklet will examine some specific questions that can bring the spiritual challenges of a story to the surface. It is not a call to analyse rather than enjoy. It is a call to enhance the enjoyment through noticing and connecting. These questions can be asked of any story. Examples in this booklet will be drawn from several books and films. Hopefully some, if not all, will be familiar to those who read this.

Here is the set of questions I propose for this exploration.

1. Does anyone in this story play a Christ-like role?
2. What does the story say about good and evil?
3. What does the story say about relationships and self-worth?
4. Is there a sense of 'otherness'?

Before we use the questions it is appropriate to explain why these particular four are useful.

---

1   Publicity Leaflet *'Spirituality in the Diocese of Canterbury.'*

1. Does Anyone in This Story Play a Christ-like Role?

The first question springs from a Christian understanding of spirituality and of Jesus. Spirituality is a popular word at the moment, but it carries very different meanings in different contexts. Sometimes it is used in the sense of the 'inanimate or intellectual part of a person.'[2] Sometimes it is used specifically with reference to God. Sometimes it describes all things in between, including a vague (but real) sense that there is something or someone 'out there' beyond the physical. For the Christian, spirituality is to do with God. If someone has a positive spiritual experience then it must be God at work—where else can it have come from? The Christian notes that Jesus said he is the way, the truth and the life and that no one comes to the Father except through him (John 14.6). For the Christian—someone who believes and trusts in Jesus—spirituality is focused on Jesus, not at the expense of a focus on the whole Trinity, but in acknowledgement that he is 'the door' (John 10.7). Thus it would be surprising and lacking if a discussion of spirituality did not include the question: 'Are there useful insights here about Jesus?'

2. What Does the Story Say About Good and Evil?

The second question is the working out of our desire to live in obedience to Christ. Part of this is the developing ability to recognize good and evil and to analyse behaviour and motives. When Paul encouraged the Christians in Philippi to pursue all that is lovely, honourable and pure (Phil 4.8) he was assuming that they understood what such things might look like. He concluded by suggesting that they look at his life—in a sense, reading the story that they saw there. Decisions, characters and behaviour in stories challenge us to think about what we believe to be good or evil, and what criteria we are using as we make such judgments.

3. What Does the Story Say about Relationships and Self-worth?

The second great commandment is to love one's neighbour (Matt 22.39). Good and bad relationships are modelled by other people in real life and in fiction. It is difficult to think of a story that does not focus on, or have as an underlying theme, the development of relationships between the characters. In real life it is not always easy to get relationships right. Fictional situations can offer new insights as examples of communication and motivation are portrayed.

And we are to love our neighbour *as we love ourselves.* Part of our spirituality is a developing understanding of what it is to be made in the image of God. Our perception of the value of a human person lies at the heart of many ethical and behavioural issues. Through the centuries it has been argued in

---

2   *Concise Oxford Dictionary*, 7th Ed (Oxford: University Press, 1983).

different contexts that one sort of human is less valuable than another. Definitions and labels of race, religion, handicap and wealth have all been used as tools to diminish someone's worth.

In current western society there is—rightly—much discussion about 'self-esteem.' The traditional Christian teaching is that our worth and value come from the fact that we are made in the image of God and loved by him. It is about God's grace; it does not depend on achievement, looks or background. From stories we can recognize the situations in which this respect and self-respect can develop. We note how encouragement can be given and received. We can follow the good examples and avoid the bad.

4. Is There a Sense of 'Otherness'?

The fourth question is based on the biblical theme, summed up in Jesus' statement, that the kingdom of God is not of this world (John 18.36). If a story has no reference at all to a longing or yearning for something outside the physical and material, then any elements of Christian spirituality it contains are likely to be limited. This longing can be expressed in very different and unexpected ways. Sometimes the experience of 'otherness' breaks through into the day-to-day life of characters.

We are called to be doers as well as hearers. We are called to grow, not just to read. There is thus an underlying question behind the four mentioned above: *What difference does this make to my life?* This needs to be constantly intermingled with the other questions.

2
The Questions Deployed

1. Does Anyone in This Story Play a Christ-like Role?

Before asking this of our story, an important prior question to ask of ourselves is: What images do we already have of Christ? Despite increasing secularization it is a fair assumption that most people in our society, whether Christian or not, have heard of Jesus. They may know next to nothing. They may know a great deal. And when they hear the name, different images will inevitably come to mind.

The image may be of a bearded man in a long white cloak. It may be of a distant, invisible friend. Perhaps it is of a baby in a manger. It may be nothing except the musty feel of the church in the next street. Perhaps it is a feeling as we receive the bread and wine at communion. The list is long and varied. Picture books, lessons at school and paintings all give glimpses. Some will have read the accounts in the Bible. Some may be relying on words heard during church services. We are different people and we each have our own experiences and backgrounds. The physical act of crossing the threshold of a church does not magically replace false impressions with true. Thus it is good to ask questions such as these: What do I think Jesus is like? Where do these impressions come from? When did I last think about this? What does it say about my spiritual roots and experiences? Is the impression accurate? How do I know? Does my cultural background make a difference?

These can be disturbing questions. A continual theme of the gospel accounts is that people did not recognize Jesus as the Messiah ('He came to that which was his own, and his own did not receive him,' John 1.11) because their image of a Messiah was at variance with the real thing. Throughout history one of the disturbing features of art has been the challenging of existing assumptions about Christ. Caravaggio's painting 'The supper at Emmaus' in 1601 presents a vibrant, beardless Jesus, which caused much consternation and shock. In recent times Christ has occasionally been portrayed as a woman. This is helpful to some, distasteful to some, inaccessible to others and uncomfortable probably to all. Underlying all the reactions are the basic questions 'What do I think Jesus is really like?' and 'What is the authority for my thoughts?'—and then, 'How well do I know my Bible?'

Turning to the Question...

The world, or a large area of the world, is in great danger. An evil despot, with psychotic criminal tendencies, has mastered a technological power which enables him to hold the world to ransom. James Bond infiltrates the evil empire, but is detected or betrayed. The forces of freedom launch a frontal attack, which is doomed to failure unless Bond can complete one final act of sabotage. At the last moment he succeeds; the attack triumphs, evil is destroyed, and so Bond saves the world. This (more or less) is the plot of all the James Bond films.[3] Bond is certainly a *saviour* figure, but is he a *Christ* figure? He defeats evil. His actions protect the weak (by and large). He is willing to risk death and accepts great sacrifices as part of his mission. He has deep moral principles—loyalty, justice and commitment to the cause. But there are contrasts. James Bond wins by strength and power. The victory of Jesus was through weakness and defeat. Surely, we might say, no one would confuse James Bond with Jesus Christ. But perhaps we are tempted to wish to see Jesus as a suave and sophisticated figure. We want it to be fashionable to be a Christian. It may disturb and challenge us that a man talking to a Samaritan woman, a man touching lepers, a man dying on a cross is not fashionable—or, to put it positively, redefines what it is to be strong.

This question: 'Do we want a "cool" Christ?' is an important challenge for some. It not only reflects on our faith but also on our behaviour and self-image.

Most readers or filmgoers would not turn to James Bond for an example of Christ-like qualities but many Christians do turn to C S Lewis' creation, the lion Aslan in the Narnia stories.[4] We shall now look at this example in some depth.

Narnia is a country in another world. The history of Narnia, including its beginning and the end, is described in seven books: *The Magician's Nephew, The Lion, The Witch and The Wardrobe, The Horse and His Boy, Prince Caspian, The Voyage of the Dawn Treader, The Silver Chair,* and *The Last Battle.* A recurring theme in the stories is the struggle between good and evil. Children from our world go to Narnia and take part in these events. Aslan, a lion, appears at various times and plays a central role.

In several of his letters Lewis clearly stated that Aslan is a Christ-figure.[5] For those with some knowledge of the Bible—and the readers in Lewis' day would have had more than many readers today—there are several hints in the stories themselves.

But There Are Limitations...

We should note that Lewis did not insist that Aslan was an exact image of Jesus. The most obvious discrepancy is the lack of a coherent Trinitarian doctrine. This is not a weakness in the stories—it is difficult to see how any

---

3 Originally based on the James Bond books by Ian Fleming, published by Pan (1950s/1960s).
4 C S Lewis, *The Chronicles of Narnia* (Harper Collins, 1980).
5 C S Lewis, *Letters to Children* (William Collins & Co, 1985) especially entries for 1952 and 53.

such doctrine could be included without being cumbersome. But it is noticeable that the 'Emperor over the Sea' (Aslan's father) has a role in *The Lion, The Witch and The Wardrobe*, but is not mentioned at all at the end of the *Last Battle* or the founding of Narnia in *The Magician's Nephew*. In *The Horse and His Boy* Aslan almost takes on a Trinitarian form himself when talking to Shasta.

Christ-like Qualities of Aslan?

A brief list of these qualities would include the following. He suffers and dies for someone who betrayed him. He comes back to life. He is powerful and obedient. He heals. He creates a world and closes it down. He is outside time. He is just and merciful. Pages could be written on the characteristics of Aslan.[6] For the purposes of this booklet, we will briefly highlight three of them, and show their relevance to Christian spirituality.

Someone We Always Knew?

People who meet Aslan sometimes have a sense that they somehow know him already. Apparent 'outsiders,' such as the cabby in *The Magician's Nephew*, sense that they have come across Aslan before—but cannot quite describe how or when.[7]

Aslan tells the cabby that he knows him already and that the important question now is whether the cabby knows Aslan. In the relationship between a person and God, God has got there first. As Christians, we do not initiate our, or anyone else's, spiritual growth. We become part of something that is already going on. If we wish to serve well we need to pray for a humble awareness of what God is already doing. As we turn to prayer it is *in response* to the loving workings of God.

Not Cosy

When Lucy is in the magician's house in *The Voyage of the Dawn Treader* she is tempted to say a spell to make herself beautiful. The image of Aslan appears, growls and shows his teeth, and Lucy is abruptly dissuaded.[8] When Jill first meets Aslan in *The Silver Chair* she wants him to promise not to do anything to her. He refuses.[9] Characters meet Aslan on his terms, not theirs.

One common feature of Jesus' ministry was that he hardly ever did or said what was expected. It was impossible to label or pigeonhole him. This can be rather frustrating for us (as it was for many people at the time). If we

---

6   See, for example, Peter J Shakel, *Reading with the Heart: The Way into Narnia* (Eerdmans, 1979) or Martha C Sammons, *A Guide through Narnia* (Harold Shaw, 1979).
7   *The Magician's Nephew*, Ch 11.
8   *The Voyage of the Dawn Treader*, Ch 10.
9   *The Silver Chair*, Ch 2.

were to write the gospels we would have Jesus answer questions in a nice straightforward way—perhaps, in fact, giving answers rather similar to those that we would give. But he has none of it.

An encounter with Jesus means that comfort zones may have to be left behind. Sinful areas will be challenged. Hidden gifts will be brought out into the open. At one point in the gospels Jesus asks a man if he *wants* to be healed (John 5.6). When we remember that although Jesus is good he is not safe (a phrase used of Aslan in *The Lion, the Witch and the Wardrobe* chapter 8), we realize why the question does not have such an obvious answer as it might at first appear. There is always the temptation to want healing on our terms rather than on his.

Seriously Joyful

There is often a lightness of touch and humour about the character of Aslan. During the creation of Narnia he encourages the jackdaw in his moment of humorous glory.[10] In *Prince Caspian* he leads a riotous procession, including Bacchus, with the great cry 'We will make holiday.'[11]

The exhilaration of the ministry of Jesus is sometimes missed. At the wedding at Cana the miracle happened at the reception, not during the service. There would have been laughing and dancing, and Jesus kept the party going. He was a guest at the wedding—presumably he was fun to have around. And some religious people found this all very difficult.

It is helpful to ask whether our Christian lives reflect this truth. There is a time for solemnity and for sorrow, but also a time for joy, for jokes, for a lightness of touch. One aspect of heaven we can safely take for granted is that we shall enjoy it! Do we have glimpses of that in our churches and in our own spiritual lives? Joy in Narnia is not forced or intense. It happens when something good has happened and Aslan is involved.

There is an old joke of a child in church looking round at all the kneeling people. 'Who are they hiding from?' he asks his mother. If Sabbath lifestyle does not include the Aslan cry of 'We shall make holiday,' then perhaps we need to ask what our image of Jesus is, and what image we project.

The Most Popular Book of the Century

At the end of 1999 *The Lord of the Rings* by J R R Tolkien was voted the most popular book of the 20th century.[12] Unlike Lewis, Tolkien made no explicit claims to representing Christian themes. But even a quick answer to our first question (Does anyone in this story play a Christ-like role?) highlights several characters that display different Christ-like qualities:

---

10 *The Magician's Nephew*, Ch 10.
11 *Prince Caspian*, Ch 11.
12 J R R Tolkien, *The Lord of the Rings* (HarperCollins, 1991). See also *Tree and Leaf* (Allen and Unwin, 1964).

- The wizard Gandalf, who goes through a death-like experience in his sacrificial struggle against the evil Balrog.[13] This sacrifice is made in order to enable his friends to escape. He returns unexpectedly with greater power and glory than before. He has great knowledge and teaches words of wisdom. He can speak sharply and tenderly. He sees people as they are, understanding their motives, whether for good or ill.

- Aragorn, who is the true king, but only takes his rightful place after many years in the wilderness as Strider the ranger.[14] This follows the pattern of humility in the style of Philippians 2.5–11. He is a healer.

- Queen Galadriel, who resists the temptation to abuse the ring of power in a similar style to Jesus resisting the temptations of the devil to earthly glory.[15] She is contrasted with Boromir, who is consumed by the temptation.

- Treebeard, who is the leader of the Ents, tree-like shepherds of the forest.[16] The Ents become angry, and march to destroy the traitor wizard Saruman. It is a remarkable description of righteous anger. The reader is carried with it and wants the Ents to be angry, and to express their anger in the destruction of evil.

For the Christian the experiences of these characters give insights into the ministry of Jesus. The figure of Gandalf reminds us that Jesus could sometimes speak sharply ('Tell Herod, that fox…' Luke 13.32) as well as tenderly, that the battle of good against evil required sacrifice, courage and inspirational leadership. How often do we think of Jesus as 'inspirational'? He must have been, or people would not have followed him. Aragorn's patience as a ranger reminds us of the humility of the Son of God as he waited for several years in Galilee before the right time for his ministry to begin. Our society moves quickly and it is difficult to slow down. It is difficult to grasp that God is not rushed, and our calling is sometimes simply to wait.

Galadriel's successful struggle against the lure of the ring reminds us that resistance against temptation is not easy. Her defence lies in who she really is—'I pass the test,' she said. 'I will diminish, and go into the West, and remain Galadriel.'[17] Jesus' resistance in the wilderness lay in his understanding of who he was, and what he was called to be.

---

13 *The Lord of the Rings*, Book 2, Ch 5.
14 *Ibid*, Book 2, Ch 2.
15 *Ibid*, Book 2, Ch 6.
16 *Ibid*, Book 3, Ch 4.
17 *Ibid*, p 385.

For those who find the doctrine of the anger (or wrath) of God difficult, the chapters describing Treebeard and the Ents can be very helpful. The reader glimpses how anger can be justified, necessary and righteous, when the destructive power of destruction itself needs to be opposed.

These are examples of what can happen when we begin to ask the first question: Does anyone in this story play a Christ-like role? Those who already enjoy James Bond, Narnia or The Lord of the Rings may be thinking: 'But so much has been left out; he could have said this or that!' This is inevitable and a sign of a good story. There is always further that one could go.

2. What Does the Story Say About Good and Evil?

It is difficult to think of a story that does not have some element of the struggle between good and evil, however it is represented. The James Bond films thrive on this. A key feature in these adventures is that the good will triumph and the bad perish. The hero, although often appearing to flaunt immorality (especially sexually), in fact has deeply moral characteristics. He has principles. He protects the innocent. He is just rather than cruel. The audience expects him, as representative of good, to win (how long would the series have lasted if he had always lost?). There is something in us that wants righteousness and justice to win through—that in itself is an interesting spiritual and moral dynamic, and a significant challenge to the atheist.

Some Characteristics of Evil: Materialism, Deceit and Emptiness

For many, the first encounter with a portrayal of evil will have been through children's stories or films. The impressions left can be deep, and fertile ground for exploring what evil is actually like.

The wicked Queen in Disney's film Snow White and the Seven Dwarfs is one example.[18] She is cruel and vindictive. She is jealous. She deceives. She can act the part of a Queen—and she can act the part of a needy old woman. She is never satisfied—it is not enough for her stepdaughter to be exiled, she has to be killed. Her hatred leads to her own death. A higher power, lightning, intervenes to ensure she dies, just as it appeared she was finally going to win. The characteristics of evil portrayed in this film are perceptively chosen. In learning to recognize the symptoms of evil, even if at first through a cartoon, we begin to learn how to avoid it.

Dishonesty is one characteristic of evil that frequently appears in stories. This is not only to do with telling lies, but the larger underlying deceit of promising happiness and satisfaction that cannot be delivered. The witch in The Silver Chair promises comfort and refreshment for the travellers if they

---

18 Snow White and the Seven Dwarfs, Disney, 1937.

go to Harfang. The reality is that they are there to be devoured.[19] She lies. The promises of the expected hospitality are enough to make them forget to repeat Aslan's instructions. The pre-occupations of materialism can so easily lead to a forgetfulness of Christian teaching.

Temptations promise satisfaction but they do not deliver, so we seek deeper temptations to see if *these* will deliver. We are deceived and we sometimes choose to deceive ourselves: 'Surely it is not really wrong'; 'If he found out, he would not mind'; 'It will make me happy.' We forget that evil has no power to produce anything that is lastingly good. In *The Lord of the Rings* we are reminded that the means always affect the end. Thus Galadriel knows that the evil of the ring would corrupt her motives, even if her initial motivation were for good, and that the result would be despair.[20]

Evil, without the physical expression of the ring of power, is just a shadow, dissipated by the wind. There is nothing to it in itself. Despair, the final surrender of hope, is one of the fruits of evil, fatally expressed by Denethor: 'Soon all shall be burned. The West has failed. It shall all go up in a great fire, and all shall be ended. Ash! Ash and smoke blown away on the wind.'[21]

In our age many people struggle with materialism, an expression in itself of inner emptiness. The best-selling author John Grisham continually raises questions about working patterns and materialism. In *The Street Lawyer* a wealthy lawyer ponders:

As I studied my finely appointed office, I wondered, for the first time in many years there, how much all of it cost. Weren't we just chasing money? Why did we work so hard; to buy a richer rug, an older desk? There in the warmth and cosiness of my beautiful room, I thought of Mordecai Green, who at that moment was volunteering his time in a busy shelter, serving food to the cold and hungry.[22]

The same issue is powerfully explored in the middle of an Agatha Christie short story. The detective Hercule Poirot has this exchange with a nun.[23]

Hercule Poirot said gently: 'He needs your prayers.'
'Is he then an unhappy man?'
Poirot said: 'So unhappy that he has forgotten what happiness means. So unhappy that he does not know he is unhappy.'
The Nun said softly: 'Ah, a rich man...'

19 *The Silver Chair*, Chs 6–8.
20 *The Lord of the Rings*, Book 2, Ch 6.
21 *Ibid*, p 886.
22 John Grisham, *The Street Lawyer*, (Arrow Books, 1998) p 48.
23 Agatha Christie, *The Labours of Hercules* (Fontana 1963) p 231.

'Forgotten what happiness means…' This is a perceptive and sadly accurate description of the state that many people feel that they have reached. Or, as summed up by Jesus: 'What good will it be for them if they gain the whole world yet forfeit their life?' (Matthew 16.26). In our spiritual journey we have to face these challenges: Do we really believe Jesus when he says this? Do the choices we make in our lives model this? Have our preoccupations led us to forget what it is to be happy?

Some Characteristics of Good: the Heroism of Living Ordinary Life Well

In Narnia, goodness is connected to Aslan. It is a recurring feature that people are drawn to tell the truth when they are facing him. For example, in *The Magician's Nephew*, Digory unexpectedly finds himself telling the whole truth about the arrival of the witch in Narnia.[24] We note that the most effective way of characters becoming obedient is to be drawn closer to Aslan, not to be nagged at by another character. In our own lives our calling to be good is our calling to look to Christ. And if we are interested in the goodness of others we should similarly encourage them to look to Christ.

In *The Lord of the Rings* there is much affirmation of 'ordinary life.' Strider (Aragorn) describes the calling of his rangers in the wilderness as providing 'safety in quiet lands and in the homes of simple men at night.'[25] Ordinary life is most epitomized by the lives of the Hobbits. And the heart of the story is that a humble hobbit called Frodo would be called for the task more naturally due to valiant men or elves.

The value of living an ordinary life well is something that needs to be constantly stressed in our Christian lives and in society at large. The glamorous, the new and the exciting may have their place, but the challenge of living well day by day requires continued wisdom and courage. And Aragorn-like, perhaps a key responsibility of church leaders is to enable people to do this. It is all too easy for churches to burden people with unnecessary meetings instead of encouraging good, normal evenings at home or in the pub.

In *The Wind in the Willows* Mole unexpectedly returns to his home. He remembers with affection all that home means:

It was good to think he had this to come to, this place which was all his own, these things which were so glad to see him again and could always be counted upon for the same simple welcome.[26]

---

24 *The Magician's Nephew*, Ch 11.
25 *The Lord of the Rings*, Book 2, Ch 2.
26 Kenneth Grahame, *The Wind in the Willows* (Methuen Children's Books, 1971) p 107.

13

In *The Lord of the Rings* Elrond's house is called 'The Last Homely House'—a significant choice of name for a place where there is great wisdom, power and valour.

To be a hero in any of the stories mentioned is to try and do the right thing. Often this involves calling up unforeseen reserves of courage and facing unexpected sacrifice. It often involves courtesy, humility and chivalry. It may be interesting to note if all these qualities are always evident in our church meetings…

A major theme in *The Lord of the Rings* is that the right decision has to be made although the outcome is uncertain and ultimate success not guaranteed. Gandalf comments:

> It is not our part to master all the tides of the world, but to do what is in us for the succour of those years wherein we are set, uprooting the evil in the fields that we know, so that those who live after may have clean earth to till. What weather they shall have is not ours to rule.[27]

It is a tremendous calling—to 'uproot the evil in the fields *that we know.*' We are not called to do more than we are able. But what we are called to do, we are called to do well.

Many people live heroic lives. Perhaps they care day by day for a housebound spouse. Perhaps they patiently survive another tedious day at work because the family depends on the income. Perhaps they run a scout group or old folks' lunch club, week in and week out. Perhaps they give up another night's sleep to sit with a teething infant. Whatever it is, here is heroism and is vital to recognize and appreciate it as such. It is significant that the fruit of the Spirit listed in Galatians 5, and the description of love in 1 Corinthians 13, are best expressed in everyday life.

Part of the courtesy and honesty of good characters is the ability to say sorry. The lack of this ability (or the perceived lack of need to) is what ultimately makes some fictional heroes one-dimensional. In the classic western *Shane* the hero is described at one stage as 'cool and competent, facing that room full of men in the simple solitude of his own invincible completeness.'[28] Humanity is fallible, fallen and more complicated. Shane does not fit into the real world, and nor do we if we pretend to be like him.

Inevitably, evil and good are contrasted. Aslan's joy is opposite to the mentality of the White Witch's 'Always winter and never Christmas'[29] (in itself, a very accurate description of much false religion—a frozen landscape uninterrupted by real joy and celebration). Aslan does not lie. He is the one

---

27 *The Lord of the Rings* p 913.
28 Jack Schaeffer, *Shane* (Bantam, 1958) p 108.
29 *The Lion, the Witch and the Wardrobe*, chapter 2.

who creates and brings joy and satisfaction. He is the way to heaven, Aslan's country. Quite simply, he delivers. The forces of evil do not.

But we often forget these truths. In John Grisham stories we often hear about lawyers who have lost their early vision to change the world and help the needy. It has been forgotten in the push for greater profits. In Narnia, one of the roles of evil is to cause people to forget. In *The Silver Chair* the witch pretends that Narnia does not exist at all.[30]

In our lives we often live as if the great memories and blessings we have received do not exist, as if we face each new problem without our rich heritage of gospel teachings and experiences. Evil would have us forget 'the great cloud of witnesses' (Hebrews 12.1) of the Bible, through history and in our own lives. It would have us forget Jesus' promises about living water and true bread. It would have us forget the hope of heaven.

3. What Does the Story Say About Relationships and Self-worth?

From the first book of the Bible to the last, the theme is relationships—relationships between God and people, between people themselves and, increasingly as Scripture unfolds, between the persons of the Trinity. Relationships are at the heart of our lives, and it is not surprising that much of what we call 'story' is the analysis and development of relationships.

To take one famous example, *Snow White and the Seven Dwarfs* is all about relationships. There is the stepmother and her daughter, the huntsmen and Snow White, Snow White and the dwarfs, the Prince and Snow White. We see jealousy, friendship, commitment and love. We see change—Grumpy's distrust turns to affection. The dwarfs themselves could be a model for many a committee meeting. But what lessons could there be for our spirituality?

The lessons are in the ways that characters treat each other. A friend of mine used to say that he wished he had the opportunity to repeat Clark Gable's famous final line in *'Gone with the Wind'*: 'Frankly my dear, I don't give a damn.'[31] But we never truly get to that stage. Deep down, we always do care. We cannot totally walk away from a person, pretending we are unaffected. To be human is to be involved.

Snow White prays for the dwarfs, especially Grumpy (a very similar pattern is followed by Maria in the film *Sound of Music*).[32] This is a challenge for us when we find ourselves among new people, and especially if one of them is being difficult and unwelcoming. Do we become defensive and prickly or do we pray?

Or perhaps we are Grumpy, always prepared to believe the worst, rather

---

30 *The Silver Chair*, Ch 12.
31 *Gone With the Wind*, Victor Fleming/MGM, 1939.
32 *The Sound of Music*, Robert Wise/20th Century Fox, 1965.

enjoying our reputation as the negative 'realistic' character. In the story, he is softened by Snow White's love. Would we have the courage similarly to change?

In the film *Schindler's List*[33] there is a striking sequence when a red-coated girl is picked out in colour while the rest of the film stays back and white. Oscar Schindler notices her. The audience notices her and she suddenly matters. We want to know what is going to happen to her. This is a profoundly biblical theme. We are not statistics; we are people. Each one is as important to God as if we were the only colour in a monochrome world. We note Jesus' parables of the lost coin, the lost sheep and the lost son (Luke 15). In each case the emphasis is that the individual *matters*. Do we really believe that God knows the number of hairs on our heads? If that is true, it has an enormous impact on the way that we regard ourselves and on the way that we regard our neighbours.

In *Shane*, the inadequate thug Chris is treated with respect and mercy by the hero, and later repents and follows in his footsteps working on Joe Starrett's farm. There is no suggestion in James Bond films that Blofeld is ever likely to see the error of his ways (would we want him to—and if not, why not?). In *The Lord of The Rings*, Gollum's life is continually spared, and he later plays a vitally important role.

What place does human value have in our spirituality, and especially on our praying and loving? If we were faced with a Chris, a Blofeld or a Gollum, what would our reaction be? If we truly believed that every person is made in the image of God, has a vast potential, and that no one is beyond the possibility of repentance, we may treat him or her with more respect.

4. Is There a Sense of 'Otherness'?

'And they lived happily ever after…' At the end of Snow White the loving couple head off to the Prince's castle. But the castle is very hazy. Is it real or is it a dream? One of the fundamental questions of human existence is about destination. Where are we going? What are we made for? There will be some who believe that we are not made *for* anything at all, that we are a random collection of molecules. In this view, even our thought processes are the result of random chemical reactions. Thus the question itself—in fact all our thoughts and words—are worth nothing.

Breaking into this depressing mindset is a sense of 'otherness,' moments when we suddenly sense that there is more than the purely physical. And that this 'something more' is real and important.

In the middle of Kenneth Graham's *Wind in the Willows* there is a chapter all about an encounter with the god Pan ('The Piper at the Gates of Dawn').

---

33 *Schindler's List*, Steven Spielberg, 1993.

For the spiritual explorer it is interesting in itself that these themes are important to the author—that a chapter like this exists in such a book.

A baby otter goes missing. Rat and Mole go looking for him and unexpectedly come into the presence of Pan.

> Then suddenly the Mole felt a great Awe fall upon him, an awe that turned his muscles to water, bowed his head...It was no panic terror—indeed he felt wonderfully at peace and happy...He knew it could only mean that some august Presence was very, very near. "Afraid?" murmured the Rat, his eyes shining with unutterable love, "Afraid! Of Him. O, never, never! And yet—and yet—O, Mole, I am afraid!"[34]

This is not only about worship in its description of joy and awe. It is also about deep longing. Mole and Rat try to hear the words in a tune that seems to dance in and out of their consciousness:

> Dance music—it passes into words and out of them again—I catch them at intervals...Row nearer, Mole, nearer to the reeds! It is hard to catch, and grows each minute fainter.

This passage is not specifically Christian. But it raises questions about spiritual longings and experiences: Are they like this? Should they be like this? How common are they? What do spiritual experiences *feel* like—or is that a wrong question to ask? Perhaps most importantly, how do we make links between this and a Bible passage such as this: Jesus answered, 'Everyone who drinks this water will be thirsty again, but whoever drinks the water I give him will never thirst' (John 4.13-14).

The words from *The Wind in the Willows* suggest something very similar to those that C S Lewis was later to use in his sermon 'The Weight of Glory' in Oxford, 1941. Here he speaks of the experience of human longing:

> We cannot tell it because it is a desire for something that has never actually appeared in our experience. (It is) only the scent of a flower we have not found, *the echo of a tune we have not heard*, news of a country we have never yet visited [italics mine].[35]

In Lewis' *The Last Battle* there dawns the realization that all that was good in Narnia is found as part of the greater reality of heaven, Aslan's country. The unicorn cries:

---

34 *The Wind in the Willows*, p 130.
35 C S Lewis, *Screwtape Proposes a Toast* (Fontana, 1983) p 98.

I have come home at last! This is my real country! I belong here. This is the land I have been looking for all my life, though I never knew it till now. The reason why we loved the old Narnia is that it sometimes looked a little like this.[36]

Lewis believed that this inner desire already exists, expressing Augustine's famous prayer 'You have made us for yourself, O Lord, and our hearts are restless until they find their rest in you.'

There is a striking section in *The Lion, the Witch and the Wardrobe* when Spring breaks through into the witch's frozen landscape.[37] Aslan's rule is not distant; it is beginning to be present now. Theologians sometimes speak of 'inaugurated eschatology'—the coming of the kingdom of God has been introduced by Christ but is not yet complete. Glimpses of the kingdom, of the 'other,' are present and are worth noticing. The witch knew it marked the end of her rule. Edmund sensed it might mean freedom.

What are we to make of this? It means we remember that people may already be very aware that there is something—or someone—beyond material experience. They may well remember specific moments in their lives when they felt they had a glimpse of this greater joy and reality. The 'otherness' is breaking through. (A parent will laugh at you if you tell them that their relationship with their new born baby is simply an interaction of a bunch of chemicals—they are aware that something much deeper is going on.) Buried in people's pasts there may be private moments of inexpressible joy. It means that coming to faith is like coming home. People do not have to throw out the past in order to face the future with God. Rather, they can be encouraged to recognize and value those parts of the past that spoke most clearly of God, and to name them as being from God.

There will be times when our Christian journey is uncomfortable and uncertain, but the destination is home, with all the comfort that this implies. The gospel is not something alien, thrust upon us from outside. It is where we belong. The 'real world' is not 'secular'; it is the kingdom of God.

'They lived happily after.' It says something significant about us, our desires for life, and our hopes for the future, that we want them to.

In the pages above we have seen examples of asking specific questions of stories. There is much more that could have been said. For those who have read the books I hope that the above will have been in some measure frustrating—that further as yet unexplored ideas kept bubbling up. The sign of a good book is that the inferences and connections go very deep. It is rightly difficult to stop the flow of lessons learnt or challenges to be faced.

36 C S Lewis, *The Last Battle*, p 161.
37 *The Lion, the Witch and the Wardrobe*, Ch 11.

3
Running Off in All Directions

Before drawing some conclusions here are two examples of one more method, the tangential or lateral approach to reading. This involves noticing a particular incident or sentence and running with it wherever the imagination might lead. It needs to be done light-heartedly; otherwise it becomes intense and over-contrived. But some unexpected and useful thoughts can emerge.

Example 1—To Survive is to Succeed...

There is a cricket book called *Ten Great Innings* by Ralph Barker. One chapter describes the great 100 scored by Jack Hobbs against the Australians in 1926. At one point the author writes: 'Seldom before or since has maiden over after maiden over been celebrated by the enthusiastic applause *for the batsman.*'[38] Jack Hobbs is in defensive mood. If he can avoid getting out he knows his team might win. At this point he does not look to score runs. The state of the wicket and the accuracy of the bowling preclude that. He simply needs to survive. Patient survival may not look very exciting, but it is going to ensure victory when the time is right.

Sometimes we are battered. Conditions are against us and the attack is hostile. We may feel that we can do very little. But if we can survive, if we can weather the storm, we are succeeding. Tears may come in the night, but joy will come in the morning (Ps 30.5). Paul reminds us that we put on the full armour of God 'so that when the evil day comes you may be able to stand your ground, and after you have done everything, to stand' (Eph 6.13).

Example 2—Cleaning Swords...

Having killed the wolf in *The Lion, The Witch and The Wardrobe*, Peter is reminded twice of the importance of cleaning his sword after a battle.[39]

We are sometimes not very good at cleaning our swords after our struggles. If we are burdened by old conflicts and half-remembered blood we will fight the next battle less well. The strength we are given is to be used afresh.

Moving on from the past while valuing memories is to achieve a difficult balance. In Narnia it is something that particularly happens when Aslan is around. It is in the looking at him that strength and wisdom come to see things in perspective. Jesus is the same yesterday, today and forever. In our relationship with him, past, present and future fall into the right place.

---

38 Ralph Barker, *Ten Great Innings* (Chatto and Windus, 1964) p 19.
39 *The Lion, the Witch and the Wardrobe*, Ch 12.

4
Conclusion

Before taking the four questions I have outlined and applying them to stories you know, we need to address three important issues.

Firstly, should we be thinking about 'Christ-like characteristics' in characters we find in fiction? It may be objected that this is almost blasphemous, since any character we find in fiction will be but a pale imitation of Jesus as he is depicted in Scripture. Moreover, why should we focus on these characters and stories when we have the 'real thing' in the Bible? Should we not simply pay more attention to this?

The second kind of issue is related, but more general. It is fair to ask whether this kind of engagement with story is valuable in leading people to think about Christianity. For if it is not, then it may be distracting us from something more important.

The third issue is more personal, and has to do with our own lives and stories. Is there anything useful in these four questions when it comes to considering the 'story' people read in our own lives?

1. Pale Imitation—or the Real Thing?

When we read the Bible, we use tools of intellect and imagination to understand what we are reading. An enormous range of factors, including the books we read and the films we watch, shapes this intellect and imagination. It is not only sermons and commentaries that provide our resource bank. Looking at stories with questions such as these four mentioned above helps to sharpen our thinking when we come to look at the Bible itself.

It is a two-way process. The stories can help give insights into life and faith. The Bible gives insights into the stories. If we are looking at stories for guidance in Christian living, what criteria do we use to assess them? The Bible is the agreed, authoritative reference point for churches across the world and throughout the ages. If we take the challenges in stories seriously, we are not called to measure portrayal of Christian themes against our own emotions—'did we like the values expressed in book?'—but against our (and the church's) understanding of the biblical record. In fact, the more we know the Bible the more we will appreciate and enjoy the Christian themes. We only recognize Aslan's equivalent of Gesthemane because we know of Gesthemane itself. There will always be limitations. Aslan, Gandalf, Pan are not exactly like Jesus, but in acknowledging the parts that do not (sometimes deliberately) match the biblical record, we can focus and enjoy the parts that do.

It is not images but idolatry, the worship of images, which draw people away for God. Aslan or Gandalf have their limitations; neither is designed to be an exact representation of Jesus of Nazareth, and even if they were they would inevitably fail. They are to be enjoyed and pondered, but not worshipped.

We can be led astray, for example, in hoping that Jesus, or our personality, will look like James Bond. In *The Last Battle* people mistake the false Aslan for the real thing because they rely on hearsay and are no longer soaked through with the stories of what the real Aslan is like. The false can appear similar to the real. It is the true Jesus who is the true image of God (Colossians 1.15, 2 Corinthians 4.4). Human images of Jesus, whether in painting or literature, are only truly useful if they draw us to look deeper at the real Jesus.

2. Stories and Faith

In *The Testament* by John Grisham there is this wry comment about one of the characters: 'His spiritual life was a subject he preferred to avoid.'[40] That could be said about many people that we know, perhaps including ourselves. Stories can provide a useful way past this reluctance. At time of writing Harry Potter is selling well.[41] A Grove booklet will appear later this year to examine that phenomenon. Episode One of *Star Wars* drew vast audiences when released in 2000. Quite simply, people like stories. Jesus was the great storyteller. He taught using stories. People listened and remembered. There is nothing new about using stories to impart spiritual truths.

It is usually easier to lend a book of stories than a book of sermons. They are accessible. In the phenomenally successful film *ET—The Extra-Terrestrial*[42] the boy Elliot is saved from death by the visitor from another world. In saving him, ET himself appears to lose his life but then is renewed or restored— a clear Christian theme. For most people 'Have you seen ET?' is likely to be a better opening question than 'Which doctrine of the atonement shall I tell you about today?'

There is a useful example in the Narnia books. An icon of popular culture, Father Christmas, appears as the representative of Aslan in *The Lion, The Witch and The Wardrobe*.[43] Three things may be noticed. Firstly, Father Christmas is somehow more real than he is in our world. Secondly he uses magic (the tea tray appears all prepared and complete). Thirdly, he is strongly on the side of good. The witch is furious when she hears he is in Narnia, knowing that his presence is a sign that Aslan is coming. The one thing he is not is a neutral, undiscriminating, benevolent old man.

---

40 John Grisham, *The Testament* (Arrow Books, 1999) p 230.
41 The four volumes written so far by J K Rowling are published by Bloomsbury from 1997.
42 *ET—The Extra-Terrestrial*, Steven Spielberg, 1982.
43 *The Lion, the Witch and the Wardrobe*, Ch 10.

There is power here. His gifts are precious and useful, not cheap and temporary. There may be an opportunity when we can say: 'Did you know that Father Christmas appears in the Narnia books? He's a bit different there.' And the conversation goes on from there.

Of course it would be inappropriate to grab every unfortunate child or adult in the middle of a good book or video and fire theological questions or teachings at them. But it does no harm to see the opportunities and there will be times when important discussions ensue.

Stories provide opportunities to encourage people to see Christian themes in popular culture. The opening of the Disney film *The Lion King*[44] is remarkably similar to a service of Anglican infant baptism—even perhaps a little quieter and more peaceful than some I have attended! There is the marking on the forehead, and the sprinkling (in this case with sand, not water); a religious figure holds the baby up for a blessing from the heavens and the animals kneel in worship.

If people want a story full of the great themes of good and evil, sacrifice, life and death which are continually replayed in popular culture then we can point them to the life of Christ. We can go a stage further and say that one of the reasons why these themes are so popular in culture is that they are faint expressions of the reality—that *all this once actually happened,* verifiably, in history, and our God-given humanity recognizes the echo of the truth. To offer someone a copy of one of the gospels is an invitation to read a story— *the* story above all, and one which includes the depths of all others.

Some books have a clear Christian background. Others do not. But in the biblical letter of James we read that 'Every good and perfect gift is from above' (James 1.17). If we believe this, we shall be on the lookout for what is good and useful in our culture. We will have the confidence to point beyond the good thing to the one who made it, to see in an author's good creativity the echo of the Creator.

3. This is Your Life?

St Paul asks his readers or listeners to read the story that was his life. 'Whatever you have learned or received or heard from me, or seen in me— put it into practice' (Philippians 4.9; see also Acts 20.18-20). One of the deepest challenges of Christianity is the teaching that people 'read our lives.' 'By this all people will know that you are my disciples, if you love one another' (John 13.34). If our lives are indeed stories to be read, we can usefully ask the same questions about ourselves.

---

44 *The Lion King,* Disney, 1994.

- Do I display Christ-like characteristics?
- What would people learn about good and evil from looking at my life?
- What do my relationships and sense of my own self-worth say about my relationship with God?
- Is there a sense of the other? Is it clear that I live my life aware that there is something or someone bigger than the material world?

Yesterday was one page of our story. Another one is turned as the new day begins. To help us through it, may we learn to make the most of the spiritual lessons that can be found, consciously or unconsciously, in stories. And may we be given grace to live our story well.